For my dad, much-loved leader of our family pack.

– C.A

*For Tatay and Nanay, who always inspire me
to travel curiously and fearlessly.*

– B.A

This is a first edition published in 2023 by Flying Eye Books,
an imprint of Nobrow Ltd. 27 Westgate Street, London E8 3RL.

Text © Catherine Ard 2023

Illustrations © Bianca Austria 2023

Wildlife consultant: Grant Johnson
Native American consultant: Shane Doyle

With special thanks to Crow Oral Traditionalist, Grant Bulltail

Bianca Austria and Catherine Ard have asserted their right under the Copyright, Designs,
and Patents Act, 1988, to be identified as the Illustrator and Author of this Work.

All rights reserved. No part of this publication may be reproduced or transmitted in any form
or by any means, electronic or mechanical, including photocopying, recording, or by any information
and storage retrieval system, without prior written consent from the publisher.

Edited by Sara Forster
Designed by Sarah Crookes

1 3 5 7 9 10 8 6 4 2

Published in the US by Nobrow (US) Inc.
Printed in Poland on FSC® certified paper.

ISBN: 978-1-838748-56-2

Order from www.flyingeyebooks.com

CATHERINE ARD

BIANCA AUSTRIA

EARTH'S INCREDIBLE PLACES
YELLOWSTONE

FLYING EYE BOOKS

CONTENTS

8 WELCOME TO YELLOWSTONE
- 10 How Large is Large?
- 12 Prehistoric Visitors
- 14 A Mix of Cultures
- 16 Tribes of Yellowstone
- 18 Yellowstone Explorers
- 20 The First National Park
- 22 The Flight of Nez Perce

24 LAND OF THE GEYSERS
- 26 Beneath the Surface
- 28 Hydrothermal Marvels
- 30 Grand Prismatic Spring
- 32 Waters of the Park
- 34 The Water Beast of Overlook Mountain

36 WILDLIFE OF THE PARK

- 38 The Greater Yellowstone Ecosystem
- 40 Mistakes of the Past
- 42 The Return of the Wolves
- 44 Sagebrush Steppe Grasslands
- 46 Wildfires
- 48 Mountain Meadows
- 50 Life in the Water
- 52 Wildlife in Winter
- 54 Alpine Tundra
- 56 Life in the Skies

58 THE PARK TODAY

- 60 People of the Park
- 62 Watching Wildlife
- 64 Off the Beaten Track
- 66 Amazing Migrations
- 68 Wildlife in Peril
- 70 Saving the Bison
- 73 Changing Landscapes

- 74 Glossary
- 75 Index
- 76 About the Author and the Illustrator

INTRODUCTION

In the Rocky Mountains of America there is a wilderness that is so spectacular and so extraordinary that it is known throughout the world. It is a place where eagles soar over jagged peaks, waterfalls plunge down rocky cliffs, vast herds graze on sweeping grasslands, and icy forests ring with the howls of wolves. It is also a place where mud bubbles, springs steam, and water explodes from deep underground.

People have been drawn to this landscape for thousands of years. Now it's your turn to explore . . .

WELCOME TO YELLOWSTONE

HOW LARGE IS LARGE?

Everything about Yellowstone National Park is supersized. The park sits in the northwest corner of Wyoming and spreads into the states of Montana and Idaho. It covers an area of 3,471 mi². That's larger than thirty-two of the world's countries!

Mammoth Hot Springs

Roosevelt's Arch

Grand Prismatic

Grand Canyon in the Yellowstone River

YELLOWSTONE CALDERA

Old Faithful

Yellowstone Lake

First People's Mountain

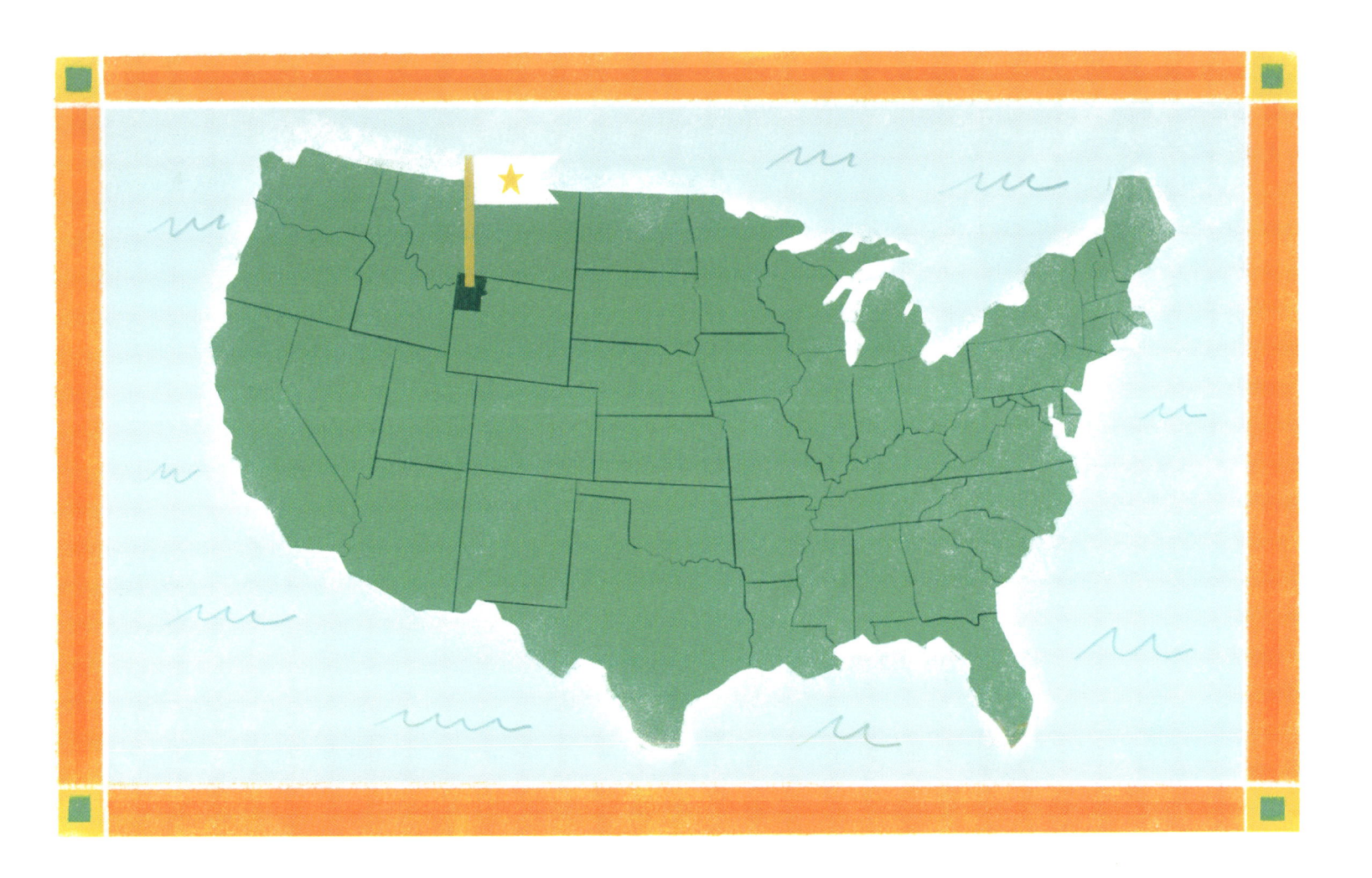

VAST VOLCANO

The park sits on top of the largest supervolcano in North America. A supervolcano is a volcano that has had gigantic eruptions in the past. The ground under the park holds enough magma to fill the Grand Canyon several times over. All of that underground heat creates the world's greatest display of bubbling hot springs and steaming geysers above the ground.

PLENTIFUL WATER

Around 55 million people living downstream from Yellowstone depend on the water supply that starts out in the forty high peaks of the park's mountains. Water from melted snow and underground springs trickles down to form streams, lakes, and rivers that eventually join up with the mighty Columbia, Missouri, and Colorado river systems.

ENDLESS EXPLORING

There are many different ways to discover this huge wilderness. You can hike along the 900 miles of trails that crisscross the park, or jump on a bike and cycle 63 miles from the north edge to the south edge. You could drive along 250 miles of roads, or take a boat out on Yellowstone Lake and explore its 140 miles of shoreline.

PREHISTORIC VISITORS

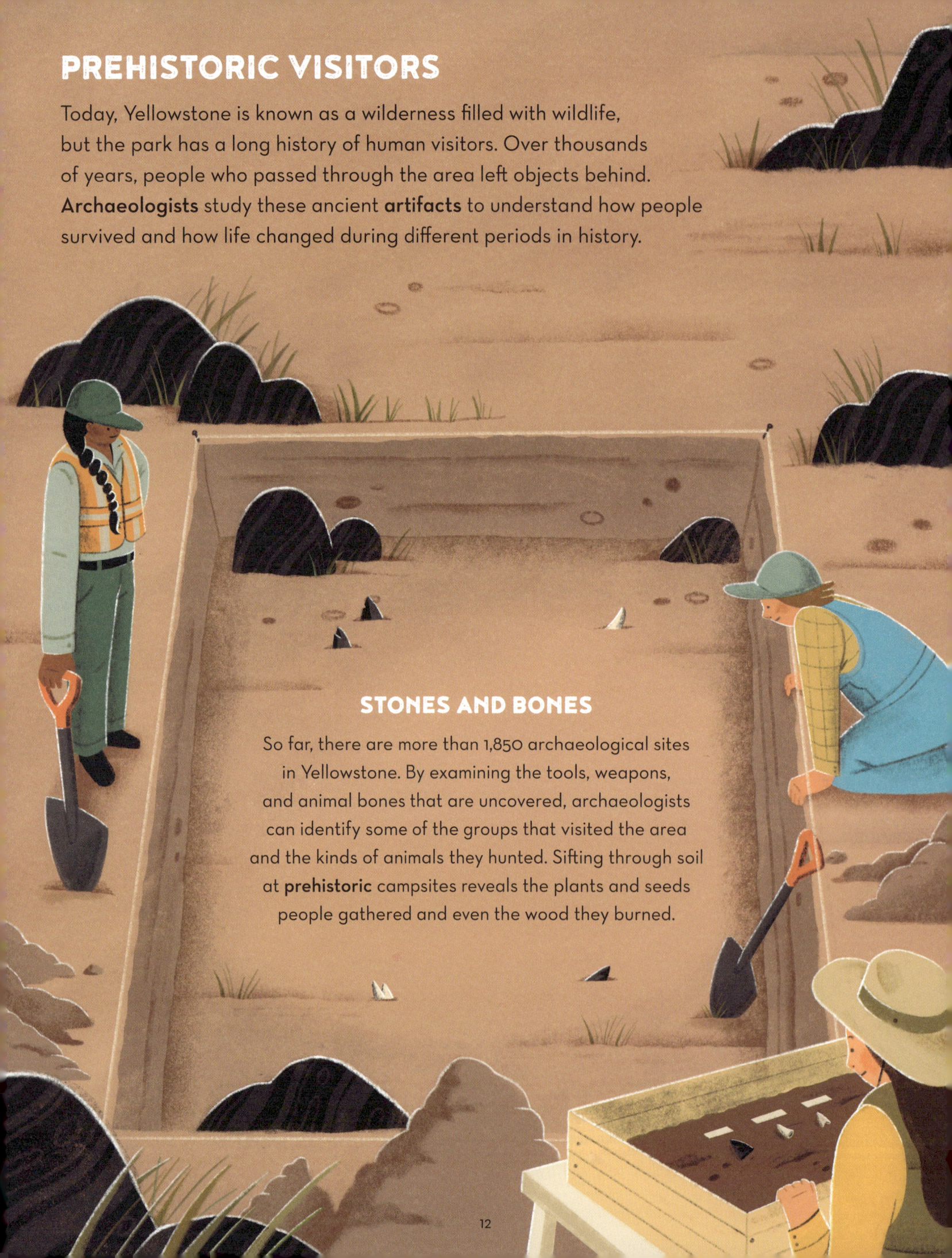

Today, Yellowstone is known as a wilderness filled with wildlife, but the park has a long history of human visitors. Over thousands of years, people who passed through the area left objects behind. **Archaeologists** study these ancient **artifacts** to understand how people survived and how life changed during different periods in history.

STONES AND BONES

So far, there are more than 1,850 archaeological sites in Yellowstone. By examining the tools, weapons, and animal bones that are uncovered, archaeologists can identify some of the groups that visited the area and the kinds of animals they hunted. Sifting through soil at **prehistoric** campsites reveals the plants and seeds people gathered and even the wood they burned.

EARLY EXPLORERS

The Clovis people were the earliest known visitors to Yellowstone at the end of the Ice Age, 11,000 years ago. These hardy hunters wore animal furs and used spears to kill now extinct mammals, such as the woolly mammoth and giant bison. Over many thousands of years, the region warmed and dried, and people came to the area in greater numbers.

LETHAL WEAPONS

Many of the tools and weapons discovered are made from a black, glassy stone called **obsidian**, which forms when lava cools quickly. It can be flaked away to make deadly spear tips and knives. It is the sharpest natural substance on Earth—and Obsidian Cliff in Yellowstone is one of the best places in North America to find it. Eleven thousand years ago, people were traveling hundreds of miles to get this prized material.

A MIX OF CULTURES

Yellowstone lies at a point where three Native American cultures meet—Great Plains, Great Basin, and Plateau Indians. Tribes from these different regions had their own beliefs and cultures, but they all traveled long distances to reach Yellowstone, a place of bountiful food, precious materials, and natural wonders.

MEETING POINT

Yellowstone could provide food for many people, so it was a place where different branches of the same tribe could come together. It was also a convenient place to trade goods and share ideas with other tribes. Large camps were set up by rivers and along the shores of Yellowstone Lake.

HUNTER-GATHERERS

Most tribes spent the early summer in Yellowstone, hunting bison, elk, mule deer, and beavers. They also caught fish and gathered vegetables, roots, and ripe berries. Some meat was dried for use in the winter when food was scarce.

HEALING WATER

Legends have been passed down through generations of Native Americans about how Yellowstone's **geothermal** features came to be. Tribes visited the sacred hot springs and geysers to hold religious ceremonies and used the waters for healing.

OBSIDIAN

Yellowstone obsidian was highly prized. Special trips were made to Obsidian Cliff to collect the glasslike material, which was shaped into spear and arrow tips and blades for scraping hides. Obsidian may also have been used as a cure for illness.

BISON

Bison grazing Yellowstone's grasslands provided visiting tribes with plenty of meat. The bison skins were cleaned and stretched and used to make essential items including tepee covers, bow strings, shields, and clothes.

TRIBES OF YELLOWSTONE

Twenty-seven Native American tribes are known to have visited Yellowstone. Stories of how they used this rich land have been passed down from one generation to the next. Today, many **descendants** of the Yellowstone tribes feel connected to this important place from their **ancestor**'s past.

BLACKFOOT

These Great Plains Indians followed bison herds onto Yellowstone's grasslands each spring. In summer, different Blackfoot groups came together in large camps for the Sun Dance—a religious **ceremony** with songs, dance, and drumming.

CROW

From the 1700s, the Crow tribe became skilled horse riders. By hunting on horseback, they could travel farther and faster. They followed migrating herds from place to place with their horses pulling their belongings on a **travois**.

SHEEP EATER SHOSHONE

This tribe adapted to mountain life and stayed in Yellowstone through the winter, sheltering in portable dens. The tribe was named after the bighorn sheep that they hunted. They made use of the whole animal, soaking the horns in the hot springs to soften them, then shaping them into bows.

BISON EATER SHOSHONE

Each year, this Great Basin tribe crossed the park from the west to hunt on the plains to the east. Bison was their main food, as well as fish in spring and summer.

SALISH (FLATHEAD)

This tribe from the Plateau region spent spring and summer in Yellowstone gathering roots, vegetables, and berries. They also caught fish, which they dried and used throughout the year.

YELLOWSTONE EXPLORERS

Yellowstone was well known to Native American tribes, but European settlers did not come to the area until the 1800s. First, it took a fashion for beaver furs, then a hunt for gold, and finally a series of planned **expeditions** to put Yellowstone on the map.

John Colter was a fur trapper who explored the region while hunting beavers.

1806 1807 1863

THE NEAR MISS

Explorers Captain Meriwether Lewis and First Lieutenant William Clark made an epic expedition across the northwest of the country. Clark came within 50 miles of Mammoth Hot Springs and although he had heard of a volcanic area from Shoshone Indians, he passed on by.

THE FUR TRAPPER

John Colter was the first European to set foot in Yellowstone. He traveled nearly 500 miles on foot, trading with the Native Americans in exchange for food and shelter. He returned with wild tales of boiling water exploding from the ground, but few people believed him.

THE GOLD HUNT

Walter DeLacy led forty men up the Snake River in search of gold. They didn't make their fortunes, but they did bring back information about the Yellowstone Plateau, which DeLacy included in a map. Since he was a respected and educated man, his findings were believed for the first time.

While on an expedition, Thomas Moran created pencil and watercolor sketches of Yellowstone's landscapes that he later turned into oil paintings.

1869　　　1870　　　1871

THE FIRST PLANNED EXPEDITION

David Folsom, Charles Cook, and William Peterson explored Mammoth Hot Springs, the Grand Canyon of Yellowstone, and the Lower Geyser Basin. The journals kept by Cook and Folsom, as well as a magazine article published about their trip, inspired other explorers and scientists.

THE WASHBURN EXPEDITION

Henry D. Washburn, Surveyor General of Montana Territory, led an expedition with a military escort. They explored Yellowstone Lake, spotted and named Old Faithful, and took measurements of peaks and canyons. They also brought back the first sketches of the area.

THE SCIENTIFIC SURVEY

Geologist Ferdinand V. Hayden's team included scientists, a photographer named William Henry Jackson, and the artist Thomas Moran. Their pictures provided proof of Yellowstone's wonders and helped convince **Congress** that an area this precious should be protected.

THE FIRST NATIONAL PARK

The United States Congress was so impressed by the reports and pictures that explorers brought back from Yellowstone that on March 1, 1872, President Ulysses S. Grant created the world's first national park "for the benefit and enjoyment of the people."

THE EARLY YEARS

The running of the park got off to a bumpy start. The first **superintendent**, Nathaniel P. Langford, did what he could, but he was not given money to hire law enforcement rangers. Next came Superintendent Philetus Norris. He constructed roads, built a headquarters, hired the first gamekeeper, and campaigned against hunters and vandals. However, to boost tourism, Norris spread the false story that the Native Americans were afraid of the geysers—a lie that stuck. After Norris came three ineffective superintendents. Yellowstone was overrun with illegal hunters, squatters, woodcutters, and vandals.

THE ARMY ARRIVES

On August 20, 1886, the U.S. army took charge. Troops enforced the rules and regulations, guarded the major attractions, and evicted troublemakers. Although the army could protect the park, troops did not have the knowledge or skills to help visitors and answer their questions.

THE FIRST RANGERS

On August 25, 1916, President Woodrow Wilson created the **National Park Service**, a new department responsible for running the country's national parks and **monuments**. As a result, twenty-one knowledgeable rangers were selected to take over the protection of Yellowstone.

PARK IMPROVEMENTS

The park was created to care for the environment. It was a coincidence that its boundaries also protected some spectacular wildlife. In 1929 and 1932 the park was extended by thousands of acres to provide better animal habitats. By 1948, the park was visited by a million people a year who came to see wildlife as well as the natural wonders. In 1955, big improvements were made to Yellowstone's visitor facilities and roads so that even more people could enjoy the park.

THE FLIGHT OF NEZ PERCE

Imagine a story of escape and capture, fierce battles, and brave warriors. It has a cast of thousands and is set on the plains of the wild west, but this is not a movie, this is the true story of the Nez Perce tribe.

By the 1870s, European settlers were moving into the Nez Perce homelands in Oregon and Idaho and the U.S. government was trying to force the tribe onto a **reservation**. In the summer of 1877, the Nez Perce fled. A procession of 2,000 horses, 800 elders, women, children, and warriors headed east in an attempt to find a new home. As the U.S. army gave chase, many members of the Nez Perce lost their lives. The survivors continued on to Yellowstone where they spent thirteen days crossing the park.

The tribe crossed the mountains into Montana, but on October 5, 1877, after 106 days on the run, the army finally caught up with them close to the Canadian border. There was fierce fighting with casualties on both sides. Nearly 300 tribe members escaped to Canada, but the rest surrendered. Chief Joseph is said to have given his famous speech,

> **"From where the sun now stands, I will fight no more forever."**

More than 450 Nez Perce were sent to Indian Territory in Oklahoma; 33 were taken as prisoners of war. Today, the Nez Perce story is remembered at thirty-eight sites in Idaho, Montana, Oregon, and Washington. Many of these sites are also marked on the Nez Perce National Historic Trail, which crosses Yellowstone National Park. It is considered a sacred place by many Nez Perce.

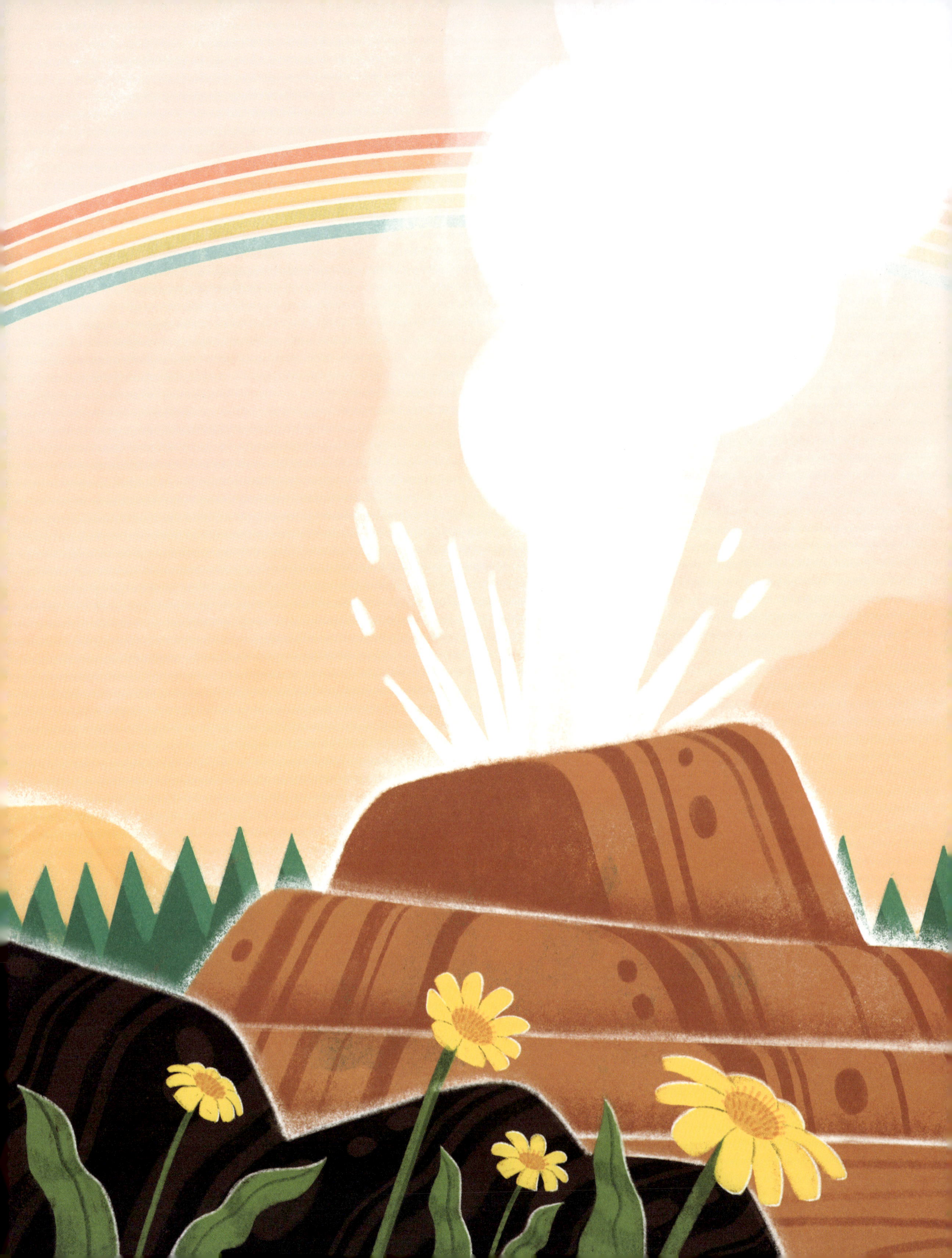

LAND OF THE GEYSERS

BENEATH THE SURFACE

Trek around Yellowstone and the ground feels solid, but believe it or not, there is an underground lake of red-hot **magma** not far beneath your feet! Yellowstone sits on the site of a gigantic volcano that is still active today. It hasn't erupted for hundreds of thousands of years, but clues to its explosive past are dotted around the park.

Earth's crust is like a jagged jigsaw made up of enormous rocky slabs, called **tectonic plates**. You can't see it or feel it, but the plates are slowly moving, inching along in different directions. About 2.1 million years ago, the movement of the North American plate brought Yellowstone over an area where magma (molten rock from below the earth's crust) lies close to the surface of the earth. This is why the area is a hot spot of volcanic activity.

When Yellowstone's volcano last erupted 600,000 years ago, it created a city-size crater called a **caldera** 45 miles by 30 miles wide. Much of the park sits inside the caldera. In places, pools of nearly molten rock lie just a mile or so underground. Rain and melted snow that seep down into the ground are superheated by the fiery rock, creating **hydrothermal features** such as piping hot springs, bubbling mud, and explosive jets of steam.

1

About 600,000 years ago a column of hot magma rose toward the surface, forming a huge chamber of magma.

2

As the chamber filled, it pushed upward toward the surface. Cracks began to form allowing the magma to escape.

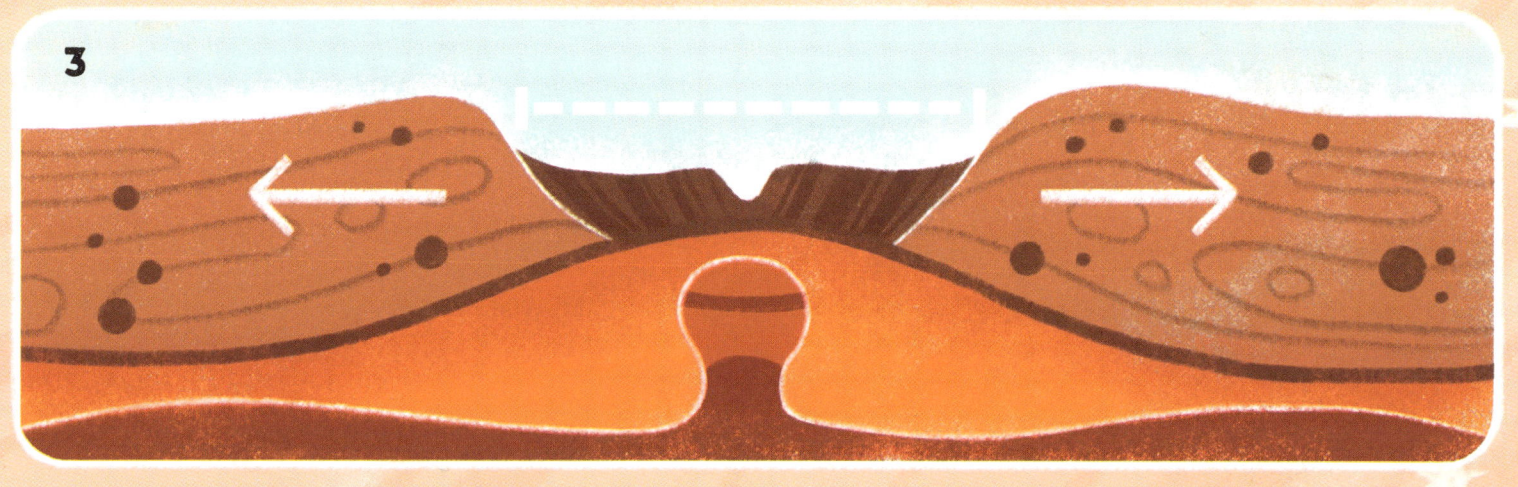

3

As the chamber emptied, the roof of the dome collapsed forming a large depression called a caldera.

HYDROTHERMAL MARVELS

Yellowstone has more than 10,000 hydrothermal features, making it the largest collection in the world. They are created when water meets rock that has been heated by magma beneath Earth's surface. Rainwater and melted snow collect deep underground in cracks and channels. The scalding rock superheats the water, which travels up the natural "vents" to the surface.

Yellowstone's hydrothermal features are all made by superheated water, but the different types of underground channels make the water escape in a variety of different hissing, steaming, and bubbling ways.

MUDPOTS

When the heated water contains sulfuric acid it breaks rock down into mud and clay. This gloopy mixture creates bubbling, burping puddles that sometimes smell of rotten eggs.

HOT SPRINGS

Water normally flows down pipes, not up them! This changes when water is heated. It becomes less dense, so it rises. Hot springs occur where the underground rock channels allow the heated water to move up to the surface easily. Although hot springs are constantly being topped off from below they don't often overflow. This is because the heat escapes at the surface, the water cools and sinks down to start the cycle again.

Rainwater collects underground.

GEYSERS

Geysers spew spectacular fountains of steam and water into the air. Geysers are created when there are blockages in the natural underground channels. Narrow openings stop the superheated water from flowing freely to the surface where the heat can escape. It collects in underground pockets and the pressure builds up. Eventually, a column of steam and water explodes into the air, then dies down and the process begins again.

FUMAROLES

Fumaroles, or steam vents, are the hottest hydrothermal features in the park, with temperatures as high as 280°F. They occur when there is so little water in the channels that it boils away before reaching the surface. Some fumaroles hiss or whistle as they blow off steam!

GRAND PRISMATIC SPRING

Grand Prismatic Spring is the largest hot spring in Yellowstone—and the whole of the United States. It gets its name from a prism, an object that can split light into all of its different colors. The Grand Prismatic Spring's beautiful rainbow waters turn from indigo in the middle to orangey-red on the pool's edge.

COOL COLORS

The heated hydrothermal water in the spring rises from deep underground, then it begins to cool as it spreads out across the surface of the pool, creating distinct bands of different temperature waters—and different bands of color. This colorful display is created by trillions of microscopic bacteria and algae living in the water!

BOILING WATER

The bubbling water in the middle of the spring can reach temperatures of up to 189°F. This is too hot for most living things to survive, so the waters in the center of the spring are a clear, deep blue.

| 95-122°F | 122-162°F | 104-174°F | 172-189°F |

HEAT-LOVERS

As the water spreads out from the center, it cools enough for microscopic bacteria to survive. These organisms are called **thermophiles**, which means "heat-lovers." Each band is a different color because it is home to thermophiles that thrive at that particular temperature. Thermophiles are too tiny to see with the naked eye, but when trillions are grouped together, they appear as dots of color.

LIFE IN SPACE

Yellowstone's hydrothermal features are studied today by scientists searching for life in space. If thermophiles are able to survive in extreme environments on Earth, they might also exist in similar conditions on other planets in our Solar System.

WATERS OF THE PARK

Water is everywhere in Yellowstone. It gushes from waterfalls, roars down rivers, and laps on lake shores. The water is on a journey that starts in the mountains as snow and ends in the ocean. It provides food and homes for wildlife in the park, and farther downstream, water for crops, and supplies for towns and cities.

Human visitors enjoy the waters of the park, kayaking on the lake and fishing along the calmer stretches of rivers.

YELLOWSTONE LAKE

Among the park's 600 ponds and lakes, Yellowstone Lake is the largest—and the biggest mountain lake in North America. It is roughly 20 miles long and 14 miles wide. Beneath the surface, parts of the lake floor boil with hot springs, but the lake water remains cold. Storms and winds whip up waves in the warmer months and thick ice covers its surface from December to May.

WATERFALLS

Yellowstone has forty-five named waterfalls. There are hundreds more without names and maybe even some yet to be discovered. Streams and rivers flow from high to lower ground in a variety of spectacular ways.

Plunge waterfalls drop vertically over the edge of a towering cliff face.

Horsetail waterfalls fan out as water rushes over a steep slope.

Cascades tumble one after another in a series of frothing falls.

YELLOWSTONE RIVER

Yellowstone is the longest river without a dam in the United States. It flows through the park, feeding into and out of Yellowstone Lake on its route northward. Beavers and otters live on its banks, while elk and bison come to drink in the shallows, and bears and birds feast on the trout that swim in its waters.

⋘ CROW TRIBE ⋙

THE WATER BEAST OF OVERLOOK MOUNTAIN

In the time of bows and arrows, a pair of thunderbirds nested on top of Overlook Mountain beside Yellowstone Lake. Every spring, the thunderbirds had two offspring, and when they were ready to fly, they shook off their downy feathers, which drifted down to the lake. The feathers collected on the surface and the Water Beast that lived down below would see them and know that the eaglets were big enough to eat. The beast would cause a thick fog to descend, then climb the mountain under its cover and devour the young birds.

One spring, the pair of thunderbirds made a plan. They had noticed a skilled hunter called Packs Antelope down below in the valley. One day the male thunderbird swooped down and snatched the hunter in his talons and carried him up to the nest. He told the hunter that he needed him to kill the beast before it ate his young, and the hunter agreed.

First, Packs Antelope told the eaglets to shake off their downy feathers. Next, he built a fire to heat rocks and boil water, then he waited. Before long, a thick fog descended and he heard the beast approaching. The hunter tipped the hot rocks and boiling water into the beast's mouth. It tumbled back into the lake, steam pouring from its mouth. That was the end of the Water Beast, and the beginning of the vents and hot springs that hiss and bubble around Yellowstone Lake.

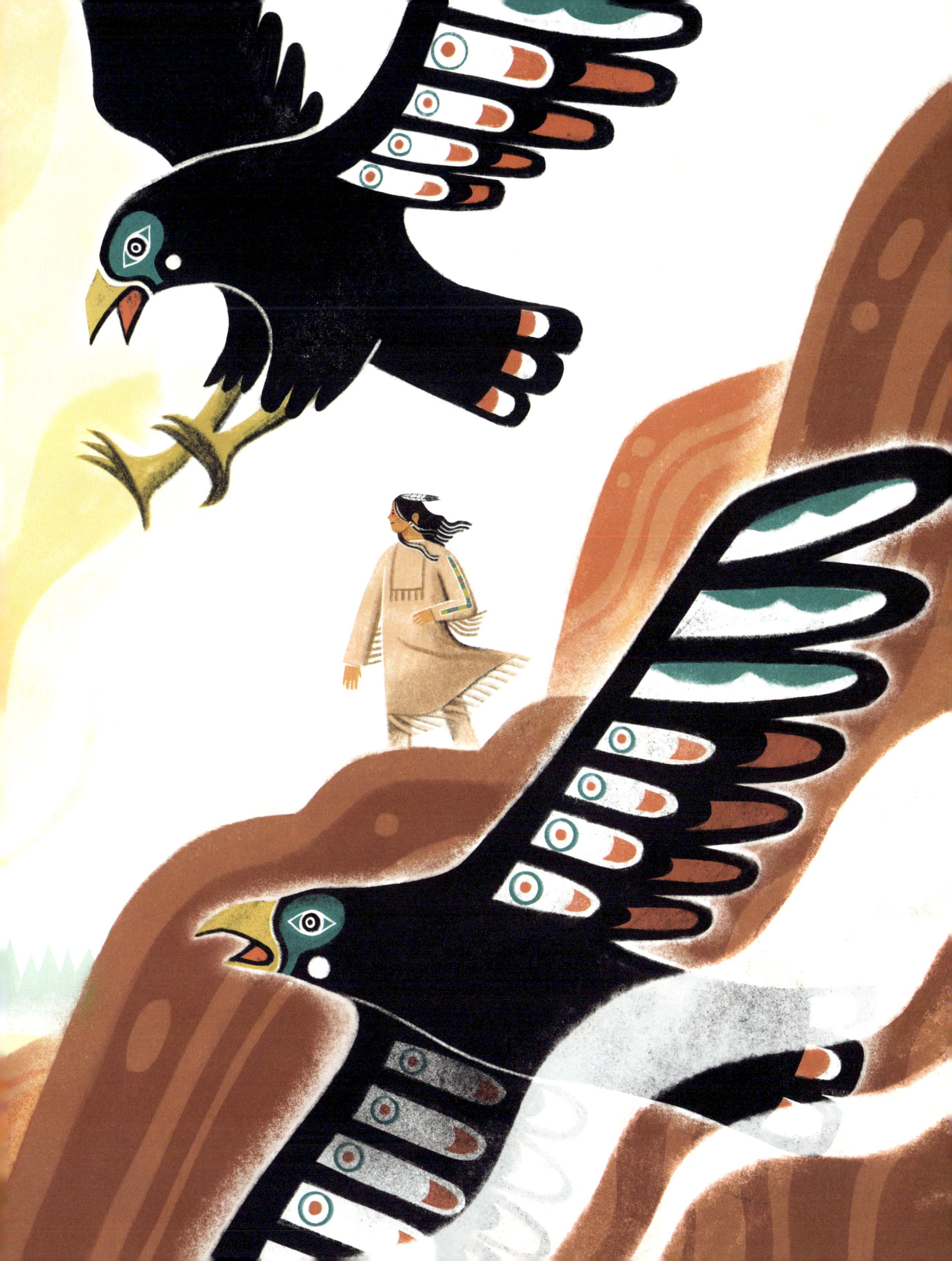

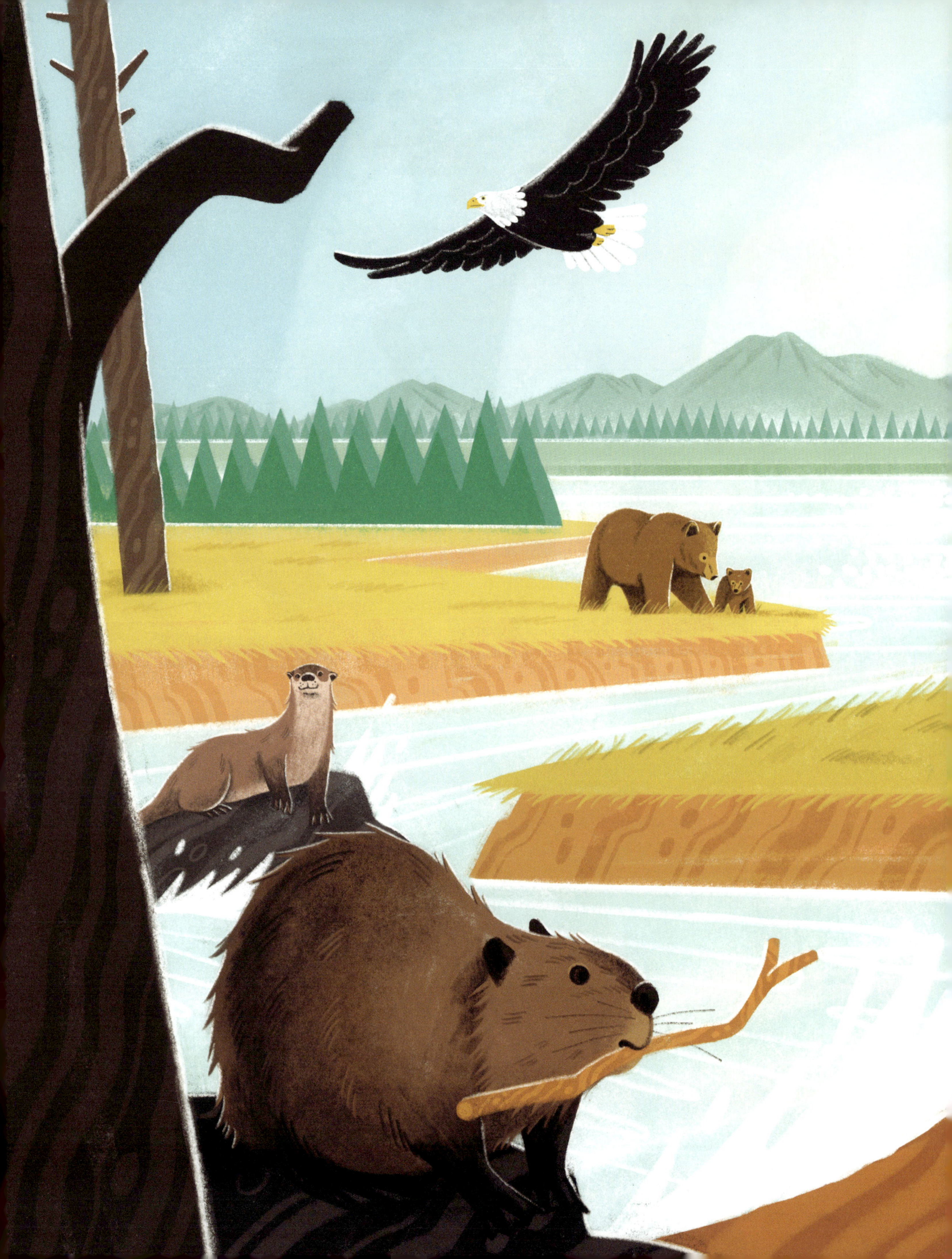

WILDLIFE OF THE PARK

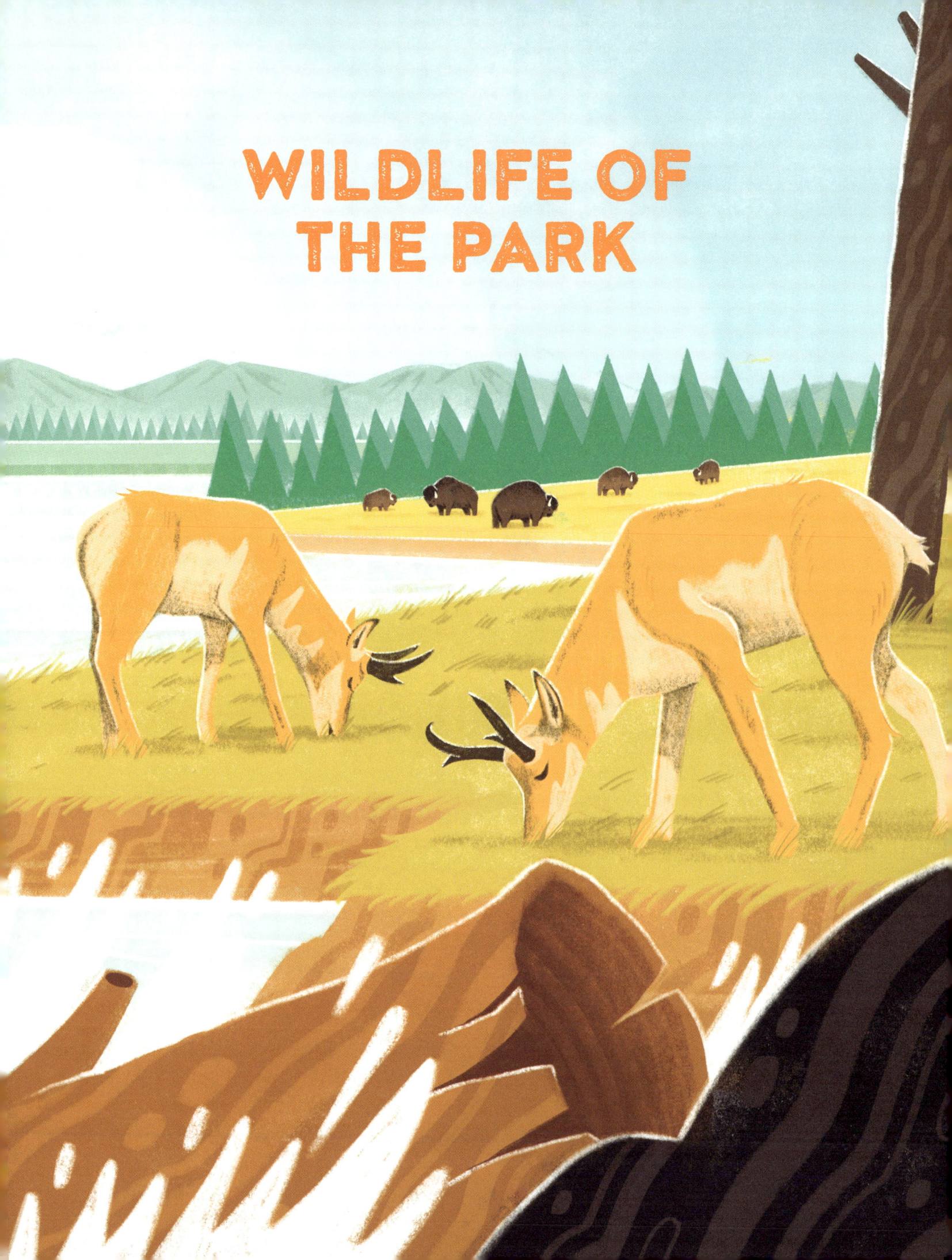

THE GREATER YELLOWSTONE ECOSYSTEM

The Greater Yellowstone Ecosystem has remained largely unchanged for 20,000 years. The huge wilderness is made up of Yellowstone and Grand Teton National Parks as well as multiple national forests and wildlife refuges. An **ecosystem** is all the living things (animals and plants) that exist in an area, as well as the nonliving things, such as weather, soil, and landscape. Everything in the ecosystem has an important role to play.

BURSTING WITH LIFE

There are sixty-seven species of mammals, six species of reptiles, sixteen species of fish, five species of amphibians, and nearly 300 species of birds in this ecosystem. The **herbivores** feed in the valleys and forests, watched closely by the many predators on the hunt for a meaty meal.

Bison and elk are the most common large mammals in the ecosystem. Thousands of elk graze where forests meet meadows, and the wide valleys are dotted with countless bison.

WHOSE HOOVES?

Ungulates (hooved mammals) are found throughout the ecosystem.

Lone moose and white-tailed deer wander by rivers and streams.

Bighorn sheep and mountain goats browse steep slopes.

Mule deer bound through forests.

Pronghorn graze the grasslands.

PAWED PREDATORS

Wolves work in teams to catch prey. A wolf pack can kill an adult elk or bison, while the smaller coyotes can catch mice, voles, and rabbits in family groups or alone. Wild cats are solo hunters. Cougars roam remote rocky regions, preying on deer, while rare bobcats and lynx hunt small mammals.

BOTH BEARS

The forests of the ecosystem are among the few places in the United States where black and grizzly bears exist together. Both catch small animals but most of their diet is made of flowers, grasses, seeds, nuts, and berries. More powerful grizzlies will sometimes hunt large mammals.

MISTAKES OF THE PAST

～∞～

From *Little Red Riding Hood* to *The Three Little Pigs*, tales of howling wolves with huge appetites have taught us to fear these skilled hunters, but as this true story will show, wolves have more to fear from humans then we have from them.

Long before humans arrived, packs of wolves roamed wild in Yellowstone; then, in the 1800s, European settlers moved west bringing cows and sheep with them. They let their livestock graze freely and the wolves enjoyed an easy meal, so fear and hatred of wolves grew. Over the next hundred years, people hunted, trapped, and poisoned the wolves across America, until, in 1926, the last two wolf pups in Yellowstone were killed by park rangers.

With the wolves gone, coyotes moved into their territory and killed large numbers of foxes, and pronghorn. Meanwhile, the elk herds that were normally hunted by wolves grazed undisturbed. They munched through the young plants and willows along the riverside. Without the willows, beavers went without food, shelter, and wood to build their dams. Without beaver dams, the rivers flowed too fast for fish to feed and spawn. Without enough fish to eat, otters and bears went hungry, and so it went on.

By the 1960s and 1970s, people realized that the wolves had an important role to play in keeping nature in balance. Many laws were passed to correct the mistakes of the past. In 1975, the long process of deciding how to bring wolves back to Yellowstone began. Eventually, in 1995, the first grey wolves were released back into the park. The wolves thrived and the natural order was restored. Today, the howl of wolves rings out across Yellowstone once more.

THE RETURN OF THE WOLVES

One January day in 1995, a horse-drawn sleigh slid across the snow in Yellowstone Park. It carried wolves brought from Canada. This was a fresh start for the wolves, and for all the wildlife that had suffered since the last wolf pups were killed almost seventy years earlier. Today, more than 100 wolves live in the park and the whole Yellowstone ecosystem is thriving.

TOP DOGS

Grey wolves are **apex predators**, which means they are at the top of the food chain. This doesn't mean that life is easy though—they can still be injured or killed by other predators and sometimes even the prey they hunt. Their return to Yellowstone sets off a **trophic cascade**—an effect like the ripples when a pebble is dropped in a pond. The wolves' arrival caused changes to spread out across the park, touching everything from plants and mammals to tiny bugs.

HEALTHY HERDS

First, the wolves preyed on the elk, bringing down the size of the huge herds. They caught the weak and sick animals, which made the elk herds stronger.

TALL TREES

With wolf packs on the prowl, the elk chose to graze on higher ground. This left elder and willow seedlings to grow in the valleys again. Some trees grew tall enough for birds to nest in once more. Beavers returned and built dams from the willow. The dammed rivers flowed slowly, providing homes for fish and pondlife.

FREE FOOD

Even the carcasses left by the wolves brought benefits. They provided a meaty meal for scavenging grizzly bears, eagles, ravens, and beetles.

SAGEBRUSH STEPPE GRASSLANDS

Sagebrush steppe grasslands stretch over wide areas of western North America, including the Greater Yellowstone Ecosystem. They are covered in grasses and woody shrubs known as sagebrush. Where it is too dry and cold for trees or lush plants to grow, grasslands provide food, shelter, and hunting grounds for hundreds of species of wildlife.

BISON

Yellowstone is home to the largest herd of wild bison in the United States. These huge, grazing beasts are the gardeners and guardians of the grassland ecosystem. Because they mostly feed on the fast-growing grasses, other plants are given space to grow, and these plants provide food for different animal species. Bison herds constantly move on, leaving their dung behind. This spreads nutrients over the ground, which causes healthier plants to grow, providing better food for other wildlife.

SAGE GROUSE

These large, ground-dwelling birds nest under sagebrush bushes and feed on its tough leaves and roots. The habitat provides plenty of insects for their newly hatched chicks to feast on until they are able to eat sagebrush too.

PRONGHORN

Pronghorn are perfectly suited to life on the dry steppe because they get all the water they need from the woody shrubs they munch. Pronghorn can also eat plants that would be toxic to other grazing animals.

BLACK-TAILED JACKRABBIT

These hares have a double set of front teeth to nibble through coarse sagebrush leaves and twigs. Like rabbits, jackrabbits eat their droppings to get the maximum moisture and goodness from their food.

WILDFIRES

It is July and a thunderstorm rumbles overhead. Yellowstone suffers thousands of lightning strikes every summer—a few of them turn into wildfires. Naturally caused fires play an important role in the ecosystem and most are left to burn. Over thousands of years, plants and animals have adapted to wildfire—in fact, some could not survive without it.

Lodgepole pines make up about eighty percent of Yellowstone's forests. They need fire to release their seeds. Forest fires clear the ground of plants and leave a carpet of nutrient-packed ash. This rich, sunlit soil provides the perfect conditions for lodgepole seedlings to grow.

The cones' protective coating is melted away by the fire's heat.

The cones burst open and the seeds are scattered.

Most animals are not harmed by wildfires, and some even benefit. Birds that nest in dead trees, like black-eyed woodpeckers, flickers, and bluebirds, have a selection of charred trunks to choose from. There is a handy supply of food, too, because ants and beetles are attracted to burnt trees.

The tops of many plants burn in wildfires, but the roots and bulbs survive. After the first rain, wildflowers and grasses appear, providing shelter for small animals and food for larger mammals like deer. Predators such as black and grizzly bears, cougars, and wolves simply move out of the way of a fire. The bears soon return to graze on the lush new plants.

MOUNTAIN MEADOWS

In May, the snow finally melts on the mountain meadows and they burst into life. A multi-colored carpet of lush grass and wildflowers provides nourishing food for a variety of animals. From the flower petals nibbled by grazers, to the nectar collected by insects, everything is edible!

Female pronghorn give birth to their fawns in May or June. The young stay hidden in the grasses while the mother grazes nearby.

FAST GROWERS

Up to 20,000 elk return from their winter feeding grounds outside the park to enjoy the feast. Males must build up their energy to grow new antlers, which start to sprout in spring. A fuzzy layer of skin, called velvet, pumps blood to the antler bones, helping them grow nearly an inch a day.

RECORD RUNNERS

They may look like antelope, but pronghorn are one of a kind. They have existed in North America for 20 million years. An adult can outrun its enemies with speeds of fifty to sixty miles per hour. Pronghorn are the second-fastest land animals on Earth after the cheetah.

HORNS OR ANTLERS?

Antlers are made of bone and are shed each year. They usually have prongs or forks.

Horns are made of keratin (the same stuff as fingernails). They don't shed but grow continuously. They usually have one point.

GOOD LISTENERS

Mule deer get their name from their big, mule-like ears. They browse the tender grass shoots and flowering plants, while listening out for danger. They can move their ears separately in different directions to pick up distant sounds.

LIFE IN THE WATER

Yellowstone's waters are home to a variety of wildlife, one of the most important of which are beavers. Today, more than one hundred beaver colonies shape the landscape with their dam-building; felling trees, diverting streams, and creating ponds and marshes that provide habitats for other creatures in the ecosystem.

BEAVER

Willow and aspen are the favorite food and building material of these toothy mammals. They chew through branches to construct dams in shallow streams. The resulting deep water is where beavers build their "lodges"—dens with secret underwater entrances to keep beavers and their young safe from bears, wildcats, and wolves.

Yellowstone cutthroat trout

Lake trout

Brown trout

TROUT

The Yellowstone cutthroat trout is the only trout in the ecosystem that is **native** (exists naturally), but it is under threat. As early as the 1880s, people began introducing lake, brook, brown, and rainbow trout for better fishing, but this led to less food and space for the native trout. Lake trout also prey upon the smaller cutthroats.

AMPHIBIANS

There are five species of amphibian in the Greater Yellowstone Ecosystem. In spring, they lay their eggs in quiet, shallow waters where their larvae can hatch and grow. Amphibians feed on worms, slugs, insects, and tiny pondlife. They, in turn, are a meal for reptiles, birds, mammals, and fish.

Plains spadefoot toad

Western tiger salamander

Rainbow trout

Boreal chorus frog

Brook trout

RIVER OTTER

River otters have thick fur to protect against the icy winters, and webbed feet and a strong tail to power through the water. They close their ears and nostrils to hunt underwater, using their whiskers to detect crayfish, frogs, and fish.

WILDLIFE IN WINTER

In winter, temperatures can drop to -40° F and a thick blanket of snow covers Greater Yellowstone. On high ground it can be piled 30 feet deep—enough to almost completely bury a two-story house! Animals have to grow a warmer coat, move on to find food, or sleep through until spring if they are to survive.

HIBERNATION

Some mammals hibernate for many months in winter. Their body temperature lowers and their heart and breathing slow down to save energy. True hibernators, such as chipmunks and ground squirrels, sleep deeply, but black and grizzly bears fall into a lighter sleep called "torpor." Although groggy, they can be ready to defend themselves in seconds if disturbed. Bears prepare for **hibernation** in the fall by putting on fat and digging a snug den. They then go without eating, drinking, peeing, or pooping from November until they emerge as late as April or even May!

MIGRATION

Many of Yellowstone's birds fly to central and south America during the colder months. Grazers, like elk, bison, and mule deer migrate long distances to find food on lower ground. They tread in each other's snow tracks to save their energy. Predators like wolves and cougars follow their prey.

KEEPING WARM

Golden-crowned kinglets are one of the world's smallest songbirds. They keep their tiny bodies warm in winter by moving nonstop, fluttering and hopping as they forage for food and search for nesting sites. At night they huddle together for warmth.

White-tailed jackrabbit

Long-tailed weasel

Snowshoe hare

CAMOUFLAGE

Some small mammals turn white for winter. Their snowy coats blend into the background, making it harder for predators to hunt them. Their winter fur traps more air, too, which keeps them warmer.

ALPINE TUNDRA

Alpine tundra is a type of dry, rocky, landscape near mountain tops. It is too cold for trees to survive, and plants grow close to the ground to escape the freezing winds. Lichen clings to rocks and grasses sprout from the stony soil. Only a few of Yellowstone's animals can live in this harsh environment.

PIKA

They may look cuddly, but these little mammals are tough! Pika spend their entire lives on treacherous mountains slopes. They hide under rocks to escape the wild weather and survive through winter on a store of grasses and flowers that they collect during the summer. **Climate change** is a threat to the plucky pikas. Their thick fur means they could overheat as temperatures rise.

BIGHORN SHEEP

These wild mountain sheep get their name from the males' huge, curled horns, which can weigh as much as the rest of their skeleton. Bighorns stay out of reach of predators by clambering onto narrow ledges and leaping across slippery rock faces. Special hooves with a padded center and a hard, outer edge give bighorns excellent grip on uneven ground.

MOUNTAIN GOAT

These fearless mountaineers in woolly winter coats can pick their way across impossibly steep slopes. Although mountain goats are perfectly at home in Yellowstone's alpine tundra, they do not really belong here. People brought goats to nearby mountains for hunting and they gradually spread to the Yellowstone area in the 1980s. Being bigger and stronger than bighorns, the goats take over the native sheep's grazing territory and eat the few plants that are available.

LIFE IN THE SKIES

Nearly 300 species of birds have been spotted in Yellowstone since the park opened in 1872. Rising temperatures and changing weather caused by global warming can affect birds' nesting, feeding, and migration, so Yellowstone's birds are being carefully counted and studied for signs of change.

Golden eagle

Peregrine falcon

Osprey

Williamson's sapsucker

Northern flicker

BIRDS OF PREY

Nineteen species of raptor circle the skies above Greater Yellowstone. Hawks, falcons, and eagles hunt small animals, keeping watch from high perches. Fish-eating osprey visit in summer, lifting slippery cutthroat trout out of the water with razor-sharp talons.

WOODPECKERS

The forests around Yellowstone ring out with the drumming of ten species of woodpeckers. They use their beaks to drill nesting holes in tree trunks. They also peck on bark to reach burrowing insects, which they then remove with their extra-long tongues.

WETLAND BIRDS

As global temperatures rise, wetlands are in danger of drying out. Many of Yellowstone's bird species, such as cormorants, pelicans, and trumpeter swans depend on wetlands for food and nesting sites.

Pelican

Trumpeter swans

SONGBIRDS

Warblers, sparrows, and flycatchers are some of the most colorful songbirds in Yellowstone. Their bright feathers and cheerful chirping make them easy to find on riverbanks among the willows, aspen, and cottonwood trees.

Wilson's warbler

Yellow warbler

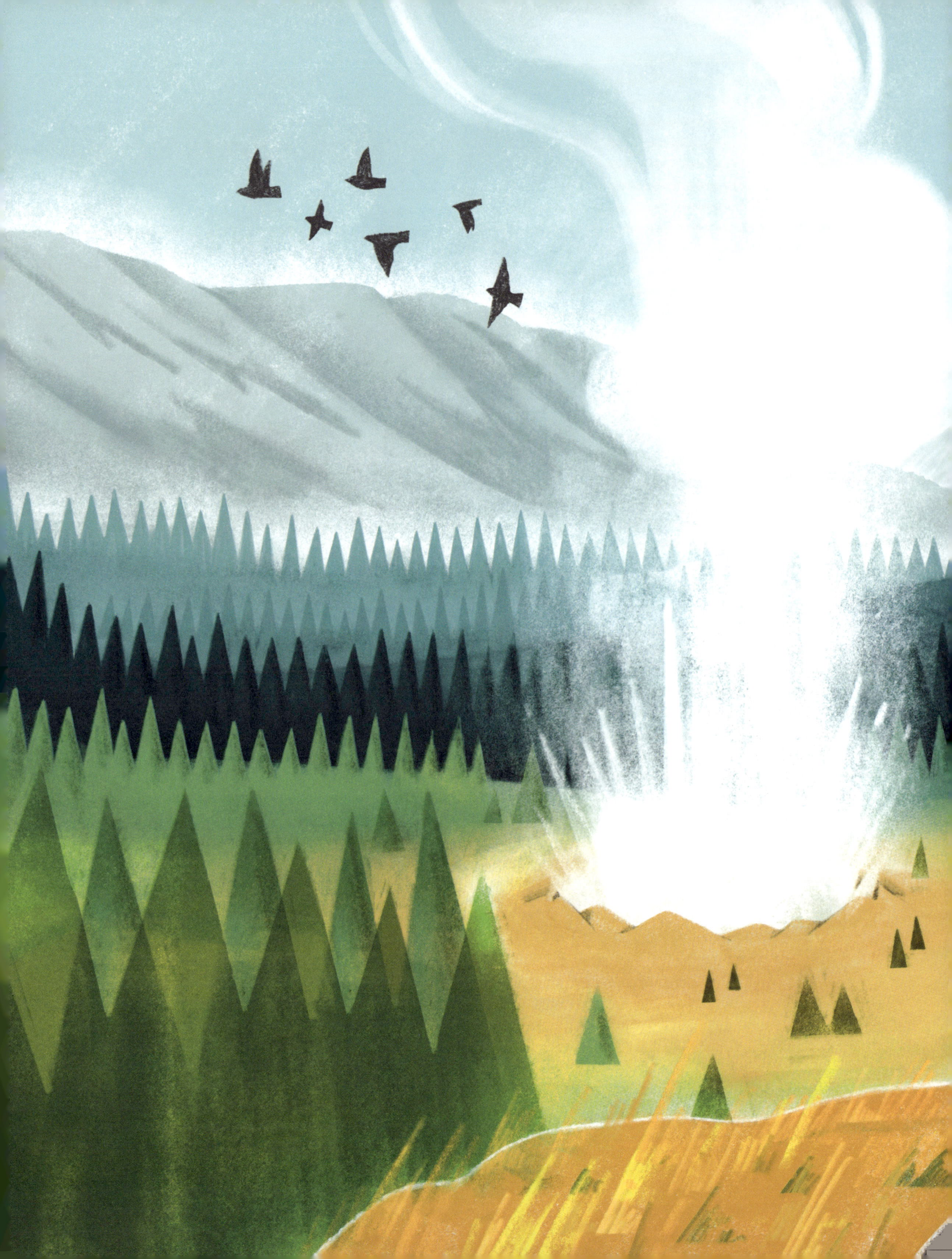

THE PARK TODAY

PEOPLE OF THE PARK

More than 800 employees work around the clock to keep Yellowstone National Park open to visitors. People do all sorts of jobs, from fighting forest fires and looking after the wildlife, to clearing the roads and delivering mail.

Rangers: Park rangers patrol every corner of the park, cruising the lakes in boats and riding along remote trails to protect the wildlife and keep visitors safe. As well as giving guided walks and tours, rangers take charge if there is an emergency.

Fire lookouts: Throughout the summer, lookouts live in tall fire towers and mountain huts to keep a constant watch for smoke and flames. They alert fire crews and predict a fire's spread by checking the wind forecast.

Wildland firefighters: Specialist firefighters manage wildfires that are a natural part of the Yellowstone ecosystem. When a blaze threatens to harm the public or property, they race to put it out.

Equipment operators: Each night in winter, operators smooth out some of the roads with snow-grooming machines, making it safe for snow vehicles to travel. In spring, snowplows are brought out to blast away the deep drifts.

Winter couriers: Winter couriers brave blizzards and snow-packed roads to deliver food and mail to park employees who live in the most isolated parts of Yellowstone.

Archaeologists: Archaeologists examine sites for evidence of the indigenous people who used the park in the past. Objects are carefully collected and preserved.

Volunteers: More than 2,000 people help out for free. "Geyser gazers" keep track of geyser eruptions. "Citizen scientists" help collect and identify insects. Other volunteers look after camping grounds, repair trails, and pick up litter.

Volcano scientists: Volcanologists study the volcanic activity in the park and predict when earthquakes might happen. Geologists monitor temperatures of geothermal features and keep the public safe.

Biologists: Scientists monitor the number of birds and wildlife in the park and study the impact of climate change. They protect endangered animals and control non-native species.

Collection curators: Curators look after books and thousands of historical items in the Yellowstone Heritage and Research Center. Displays range from old photos and Native American artifacts to a collection of old Yellowstone vehicles.

Youth Conservation Crew: Teams of teenagers spend whole summers in the park doing useful jobs, such as building fences and benches, replacing trail signs, and repairing worn-out walkways.

WATCHING WILDLIFE

Every year, approximately four million visitors flock to Yellowstone to see wild animals roaming free. There are chances to watch wildlife all year round if you know when and where to look.

Yellow bus tours have been a popular way for tourists to explore the park since the 1920s.

WILD TIMES

Most animals are more active at dawn and dusk, when they head out in search of food. April to June are good months to spot bears. They emerge from their hibernation very hungry and can often be seen **foraging** in roadside meadows. Winter is the best time for wolf-watching. Their furry bodies stand out as they move across the pale, snowy landscape.

CLOSE ENCOUNTERS

Every year visitors are injured when they get too close to bears, elk, and bison. Frightened or disturbed wildlife can be dangerous, so rangers warn people to keep a safe distance—that's 300 feet from bears and wolves, and 75 feet from all other wildlife. Using binoculars or a zoom lens is a good way to watch animals close up without putting yourself or wildlife at risk!

Bison, elk, and all other wildlife: 75 feet

Bears and wolves: 300 feet

MOOOOOVE OVER

Yellowstone's animals take life at their own pace, often unfazed by curious humans in their cars. Bear families amble slowly across roads, and stubborn bison take a break and then refuse to budge. Bear- and bison-jams are made even longer when drivers stop to snap the perfect picture!

SNACK ATTACKS

Bears on the hunt for a snack used to raid Yellowstone's camping grounds. Metal bear-proof food bins and storage boxes are now being installed to stop the four-pawed residents from feasting on unhealthy human food.

OFF THE BEATEN TRACK

Yellowstone is vast—larger than a million soccer fields put together! Only two percent of the park can be reached by road. To discover the rest, you need to leave the crowds and lines of cars behind and set off into the wilderness!

Hiking

More than 900 miles of hiking trails lead into the most remote parts of the park, passing deep canyons, plunging waterfalls, and the native wildlife.

Horse riding

In 1872, the first sightseers toured Yellowstone by stagecoach, wagon, or on horseback. Sitting high up on a saddle is still a perfect way to take in the scenery in summer.

Biking

For a few weeks in spring, the roads are free of snow, but still closed to motorists, so bikers can pedal to Yellowstone's must-see sights with only bison and elk for company.

Boating

Exploring Yellowstone Lake by boat, kayak, or canoe offers great views of the steaming geothermal features on the shore as well as the ones bubbling under the water!

Skiing and snowshoeing

Much of Yellowstone is still a winter wonderland until the end of May. Adventurous visitors can strap on cross-country skis or snowshoes and glide or trek along the snowy forest trails.

Snowmobiles and snowcoaches

By mid-December, the only way to travel on the snow-packed roads in the southern parts of Yellowstone is by snowmobile or snowcoach—a type of bus fitted with huge tires or caterpillar tracks for extra grip.

EXPLORER'S KIT

cell phone

bear spray and emergency whistle

insect repellent and sunblock

binoculars

warm layers

first aid kit

map and compass

headlamp

food and water

AMAZING MIGRATIONS

Eight thousand years ago, before the pyramids were built in Egypt, massive herds of wild mammals were making annual journeys in most parts of America. They followed the same routes each fall and spring, driven by the need for food. This behavior was passed down from mothers to young, from one generation to the next until it became an instinct.

Migration provides herds with nourishing food. It also benefits the whole ecosystem. As animals travel, their dung feeds the soil, their bodies provide food for predators, and when they die, their carcasses feed scavengers.

Big cities and busy highways have created barriers that have stopped many of the original wildlife migrations, but the wide, open spaces of Yellowstone mean elk, bison, pronghorn, moose, and other hooved travelers can still pass through.

TRACKING TRAVELERS

Research and satellite technology has recently revealed some of the routes used by animals. Each spring elk herds migrate from their different winter ranges outside the park onto the Yellowstone Plateau, following the growth of lush spring grass. In the fall, some of Yellowstone's pronghorn travel south nearly 150 miles to the Red Desert beyond the Greater Yellowstone ecosystem—an eight-hour journey by road!

Once outside the park, animals encounter an increasing number of human-made hazards and obstacles. Together with hotter, drier summers, invasive species, and disease, several of the herds are struggling. If migration is to continue, then routes need to be protected and safe wildlife crossings need to be established.

WILDLIFE IN PERIL

When Yellowstone National Park was created in 1872, its aim was to preserve the hydrothermal features. Today millions of people visit the park to see wildlife in their natural habitat as much as to see the geysers and hot springs. Outside the park, sharing a space with wild animals is not always so harmonious.

ROOM TO ROAM

Although it is large, Yellowstone does not have enough space for all the species that live there. Herds of herbivores are constantly on the move to find the best grazing, and predators need large hunting territories. There are no fences or walls around the park, so the animals are free to roam beyond its boundaries.

RUNNING INTO DANGER

Although animals are protected inside the park, once they leave, they are at risk from all kinds of dangers, such as railroad lines, fast-moving vehicles, and hunters. For much of the year hunting is allowed on the National Forest and public lands surrounding Yellowstone. Big game such as bears, elk, and wolves that roam into these areas are at risk of being shot or trapped.

TAKING SIDES

Sadly, some people are still against the reintroduction of wolves, and feel the number of predators needs to be reduced. Ranchers complain that wolves spook their cattle and kill livestock. Others see the wolves as a vital part of a healthy ecosystem. They want to limit hunting and convince people to tolerate wolves and other wild animals. While the battle continues, animals within the park at least are safe.

SAVING THE BISON

The bison is so important to North American history that in 2016 it was named the United States' national mammal. Tens of millions of bison once roamed the prairies, but less than one hundred years ago it faced extinction.

Pre-1800   1800s

LIFE ON THE PRAIRIES

For thousands of years, Native American tribes lived on the prairies and hunted the bison, or "buffalo" as many people call them. They relied on bison for food, clothing, and to make their shelters. The herds remained healthy because the tribes were careful to kill only what they needed.

"THE GREAT SLAUGHTER"

In the early 1800s, European settlers arrived armed with rifles. Over the next century around 40 million bison were killed. By slaughtering the bison, the U.S. government attempted to starve and drive away the Native Americans, whose way of life depended on the animals. By the end of the century as few as 300 animals remained.

Healthy bison are relocated from areas with too many bison to create new herds on tribal lands.

1894

1992

YELLOWSTONE BISON

In 1894, a law was passed to protect around thirty bison that had found safety in Yellowstone National Park. It became illegal to kill birds or animals in the park and the bison recovered. The problem came each winter when bison migrated onto public and private land. Ranchers feared that bison would spread disease among their cattle, so laws were passed limiting the Yellowstone herd to 3,000 animals.

BRINGING BISON HOME

In 1992, tribes from across North America came together to form the InterTribal Buffalo Council. Their mission is to return herds of bison to their tribal lands. Instead of killing healthy animals, they propose transferring surplus bison from Yellowstone and other national parks to their native prairies. So far, hundreds of bison have new homes, grazing the grasslands where their story began.

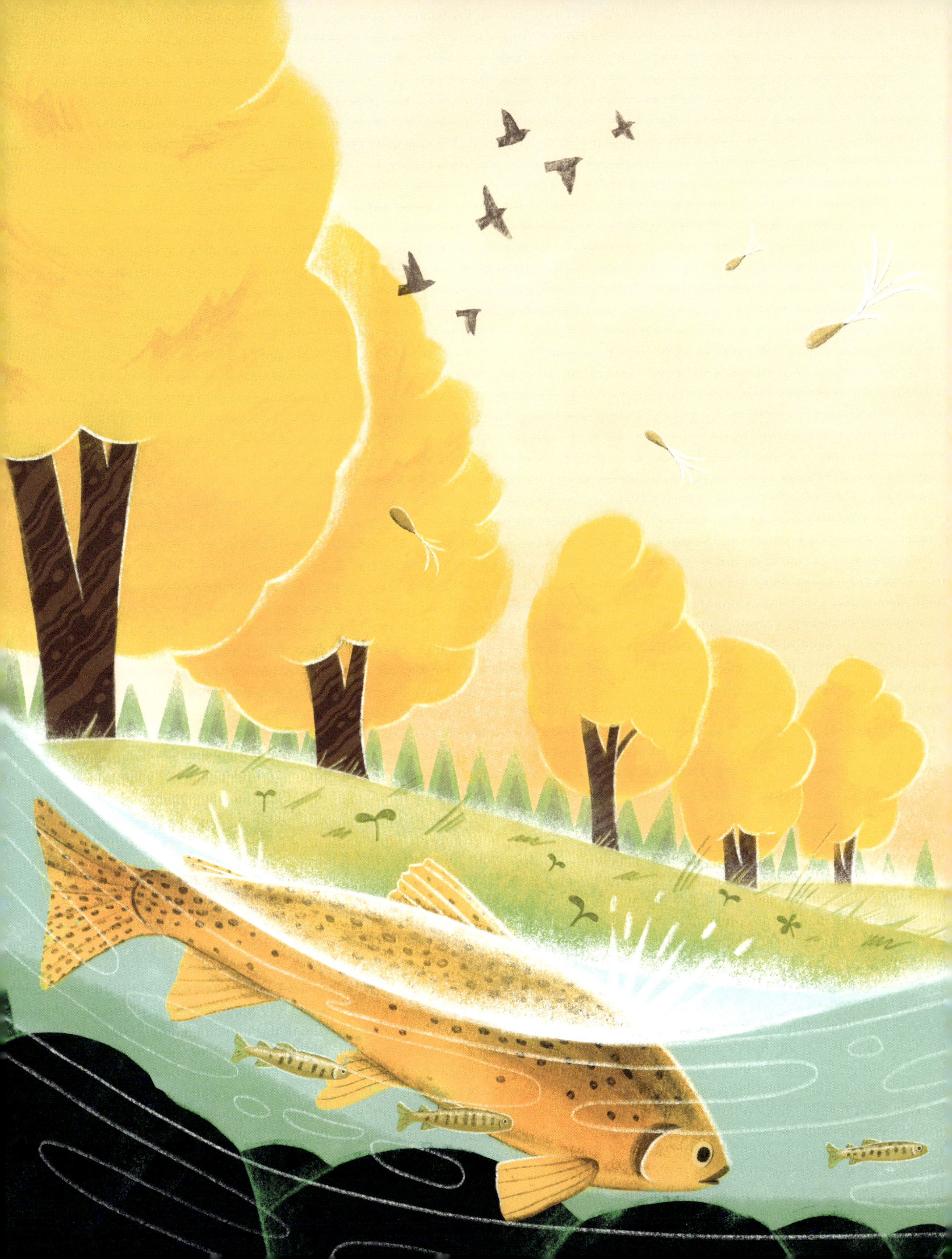

CHANGING LANDSCAPES

In June 2022, intense, heavy rainfall and rapid snow melt combined to cause flash flooding in Yellowstone National Park. Roads, bridges, and even houses were washed away and visitors were evacuated from parts of the park.

As climate change continues to cause Earth's temperature to rise, extreme events like flash floods or wildfires are likely to become more common. The National Park Service continue to work hard to plan and adapt to the challenges that the changing climate will bring.

Despite the destruction that the flooding brought to Yellowstone, nature can recover quickly if we let it. As rivers burst their banks, seeds of trees like the majestic cottonwood spread across the valley and native trout escaped to calmer side channels to spawn, demonstrating nature's remarkable ability to adapt.

GLOSSARY

Ancestor: A person who lived in the past and was in the same family as someone alive now

Apex predators: Animals at the top of the food chain

Archaeologist: A scientist who studies human history and culture by digging up artifacts

Artifact: An object made by humans that is studied by archaeologists and gives us information about the past

Caldera: A large pit formed when a volcano erupts and collapses

Ceremony: A type of formal event

Climate change: Long-term changes in global temperatures and weather patterns

Congress: The legislative body of the United States

Descendants: Someone in the same family but living at a later time

Ecosystem: All the living and nonliving things in an area, including plants and animals

Expedition: A journey made in order to do something

Foraging: To go from place to place searching for things to eat

Geothermal: Heat from the earth, such as hot lava from a volcano

Herbivore: An animal that feeds on plants

Hibernation: When animals, like bears, spend the winter in a resting state

Hydrothermal features: Habitats for microscopic organisms called thermophiles, such as hot springs

Magma: The extremely hot substance beneath Earth's crust

Migration: When animals move from one place to another on a regular basis usually to find food or warmer weather

Monument: A building or statue built to remind people of a person or event

National Park Service: An organization that cares for and preserves special places across the United States

Native: A creature that is found in a certain ecosystem and has not been introduced to the area by humans

Obsidian: An igneous rock that forms when molten rock cools very quickly

Prehistoric: The time before written history

Reservation: Land set aside for a special use

Native American reservation: Land that is set aside for Native Americans by the U.S. government

Superintendent: A person who manages something, such as Yellowstone National Park

Tectonic plates: Broken pieces of Earth's crust

Thermophiles: An organism that thrives at high temperatures (between 105 and 150°F)

Travois: A type of sled used by Native Americans to carry goods, consisting of two joined poles with a net between pulled by a horse or a dog

Trophic cascade: An ecological event that changes the structure of an ecosystem

INDEX

A
alpine tundra 54-55
amphibians 51
ancestors 16
antlers 48, 49
archaeologists 12, 61

B
bears
   diet 41, 43, 50
   habitat 33, 39, 47
   hibernation 52
   hunting 69
   watching 62, 63, 65
beavers
   habitat 33
   hunting 14, 18
   importance 41, 43, 50
bighorn sheep 17, 39, 55
biking 11, 64
birds
   diet 51
   habitat 38, 43, 45, 46, 56-57
   species 56-57
   in winter 53
birds of prey 56
bison
   habitat 38, 45
   hunting 13, 14, 15, 16, 17, 39
   importance 45, 70-71
   migration 45, 66
   watching 63
   in winter 53
Bison Eater Shoshone tribe 17
black bears 39, 47, 52
black-tailed jackrabbits 45
Blackfoot tribe 16
boating 11, 64
boats 11
buffalo 70, 71

C
calderas 27
camouflage 53
camping 63
cascades 33
ceremonies 15, 16
climate change 54, 67, 73
Congress 19, 20
conservation 61, 71
Crow tribe 16

D
descendants 16

E
ecosystems 38, 41, 46
elk
   habitat 33, 38, 41, 48, 53, 66, 67
   hunting 14, 39, 43, 69
   watching 63
employment 60-61
expeditions 19
explorers 13, 14, 18-19, 65

F
fish 14, 17, 38, 41, 43 see also trout
Flathead tribe 17
flooding 73
foraging 62
fumaroles 29
fur trade 18

G
geothermal features 15, 26-31, 61, 64
geysers 15, 20, 29, 61
gold 14
Grand Prismatic Spring 30-31
Grand Teton National Park 38
grasslands 44-45
Greater Yellowstone Ecosystem 38
grey wolves 41, 42
grizzly bears 39, 43, 47, 52
grouse 45

H
healing water 15
herbivores 38, 68
hibernation 52
hiking 11, 64
hooved mammals 39
horns 49
horse riding 64
horsetail waterfalls 33
hot springs 28, 34
hunter-gatherers 14
hunting 14, 69, 70
hydrothermal features 27, 28-31

J
jobs 60-61

L
lakes 32
landscape changes 73
legends 34
location 10
Lodgepole pines 46

M
magma 26, 27
meadows 48-49
meeting points 14
migration 53, 66-67
monuments 21
moose 39, 66
mountain goats 39, 55
mountain meadows 48-49
mudpots 28
mule deer 14, 39, 49, 53

N
National Park Service 21
National Park status 20-21
Native American reservations 22
native species 50
Nez Perce tribe 22-23

O
obsidian 13, 15
otters 33, 41, 51
Overlook Mountain 34

P
pikas 54
plunge waterfalls 33
predators 39-42, 47, 68, 69
prehistoric evidence 12
prisms 30
pronghorns
   diet 39, 45
   habitat 48, 66, 67
   hunting 41

R
rangers 21, 60
reservations 22
river otters 33, 41, 51
rivers 33

S
safety 63, 65
sage grouse 45
sagebrush steppe grasslands 44-45
Salish tribe 17
scientists 19, 61
Sheep Eater Shoshone tribe 17
size 10
skiing 65
snowshoeing 65
songbirds 53, 57
steppe grasslands 44-45
superintendents 20
supervolcanoes 11, 26

T
tectonic plates 26
thermophiles 31
thunderbirds 34
torpor 52
tourism 62-63
travois 16
trees 41, 46
tribes 14, 16-17, 22-23
trophic cascades 42
trout 50, 51, 56, 73

U
ungulates 39

V
visitor safety 63
volcanoes 11, 26, 61

W
Water Beast of Overlook Mountain 34
water supply 11, 15, 32-33, 50-51, 73
waterfalls 32
weapons 13
wetland birds 57
wildfires 46-47, 60
wildlife
   migration 53, 66-67
   protection of 67, 68, 69, 71
   species 38
   tourism 62-63
winter 52-53, 60, 65
wolves
   diet 39, 50, 53
   habitat 47, 53
   hunting 40, 69
   importance 40-43
   watching 63
woodpeckers 46, 56

Y
Yellowstone Lake 32, 34, 64
Yellowstone River 33

WRITTEN BY CATHERINE ARD

Catherine Ard studied French and English at Liverpool University and got her first job in publishing editing children's comics. She has gone on to be commissioned to write nonfiction books for publishers including Macmillan, Little Gestalten, Quarto, and Templar on topics ranging from astronauts to wildlife. She now lives in Bristol with her family and their dog Annie, where she combines her passion for books with her love of nature and the great outdoors.

ILLUSTRATED BY BIANCA AUSTRIA

Bianca Austria is a Filipina artist from the Philippines. She graduated *summa cum laude* from California State University, receiving her Bachelor's degree in illustration. She began her career working at a creative agency, mainly illustrating for clients like Facebook and Meta. She has freelanced for Disney, Droga5, and the Asian American Federation. Her work won a Gold Pencil Award in 2022 and has been awarded by the Society of Illustrators New York in previous years. She currently lives in Los Angeles with her partner and pet pigeon, Petra, close by her family.

WITH EXPERT HELP FROM

Grant Johnson

Grant Johnson has worked as a biologist and wildlife guide for more than twenty years. He started his career in the Bahamas working with sharks and other marine wildlife, and now lives in Montana working as a professional naturalist guide in the Greater Yellowstone Ecosystem for Yellowstone Safari Company. As an accomplished biologist, field researcher, and guide, he has been featured on the National Geographic Channel, Animal Planet, the BBC, and is a regular contributor to the Discovery Channel's popular "Shark Week."

Shane Doyle

Shane Doyle, an enrolled member of the Crow tribe who hails from Crow Agency, Montana, has a Master's degree in Native American Studies from Montana State University and is currently working on a Ph.D. in education. Shane also holds a Doctorate in Curriculum and Instruction and completed a postdoctoral appointment in genetics with the University of Copenhagen, Denmark, in 2016. With twenty years of teaching experience, Dr. Doyle is a full-time educational and cultural consultant, designing American Indian curriculum for many organizations, including Montana public schools, the National Park Service, and the Museum of the Rockies.

ALSO IN THE SERIES

EVEREST
By Sangma Francis and Lisk Feng

There is a place where a mountain grows. It is the highest spot on Earth, the ultimate challenge for mountain-climbing adventurers, the towering figure of Sagarmatha, the Goddess of the Sky...

Welcome to Mount Everest.

THE GREAT BARRIER REEF
By Helen Scales and Lisk Feng

In the waters where Australia meets the vast Pacific Ocean, grows the world's most famous reef. Schools of fish dart among the colorful corals, octopuses hide in dark corners, and sharks patrol the clear waters above.

Welcome to the Great Barrier Reef.

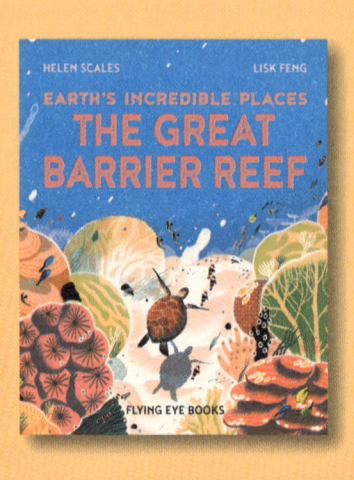

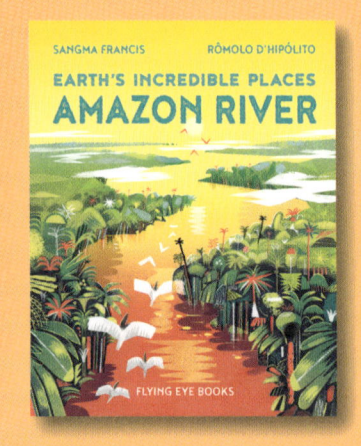

AMAZON RIVER
By Sangma Francis and Rômolo D'Hipólito

Beginning with a tiny trickle high in the mountains, smaller streams join until they form the world's largest river. From piranhas to the giant anaconda, this mighty waterway is home to the world's most incredible ecosystem.

Welcome to the Amazon River.

WWW.FLYINGEYEBOOKS.COM